T0150961

in spirit

also by Tara Beagan

Dreary and Izzy
The Mill Part 3: The Woods

in spirit
TARA BEAGAN

Playwrights Canada Press
TORONTO

For professional or amateur production rights, please contact Playwrights Canada Press.

LIBRARY AND ARCHIVES CANADA CATALOGUING IN PUBLICATION
Beagan, Tara, author
    In spirit / Tara Beagan. -- First edition.

A play.
Issued in print and in electronic formats.
ISBN 978-1-77091-806-1 (softcover).--ISBN 978-1-77091-807-8 (PDF).--
ISBN 978-1-77091-808-5 (HTML).--ISBN 978-1-77091-809-2 (Kindle)

    I. Title.

PS8603.E34I6 2017   C812'.6   C2017-904843-0
                                            C2017-904844-9

We acknowledge the financial support of the Canada Council for the Arts, the Ontario Arts Council (OAC), the Ontario Media Development Corporation, and the Government of Canada for our publishing activities.

Canada Council for the Arts   Conseil des arts du Canada

ONTARIO ARTS COUNCIL
CONSEIL DES ARTS DE L'ONTARIO
an Ontario government agency
un organisme du gouvernement de l'Ontario

Canadä

Ontario
Ontario Media Development Corporation

There is an enduring emptiness created when a child goes missing. Everything and every person is affected. A missing child is an unquantifiable symptom of the greed and corruption of society. No child should have to know that terrible behaviour is possible, yet all too many Indigenous children are subjected to unfathomable wrongs. This play is for those children who bear the weight of the ways in which this world has failed them.

In Spirit (with the working title *Quilchena*) debuted through halfbreed productions, in association with Red Pepper Spectacle Arts, as part of the 2007 SummerWorks Performance Festival at the Tarragon Theatre Extraspace in Toronto, Ontario, with the following cast and creative team:

Actor: Michaela Washburn
Designer: Andy Moro
Director: Tara Beagan
Dramaturg: Jovanni Sy
Stage Manager: Jennifer Lau

This early version of the play was later produced as part of Factory Theatre's 2009 CrossCurrents Festival with actor Paula Jean Prudat. It was further workshopped by Native Earth Performing Arts individually and as part of the twenty-sixth Weesageechak Begins to Dance Festival in November 2013.

The full production was first produced by Native Earth Performing Arts in 2014 at Full Circle's Talking Stick Festival with the following cast and creative team:

Actor: Sera-Lys McArthur
Designer: Andy Moro
Director: Tara Beagan
Stage Manager: Mike Lewandowski
Supplemental Rehearsal Director: Jessica Carmichael

The current, revised version is with thanks to the Queen's University Drama Department 2014, Gregory Wanless, Tim Fort, Adair Redish, and the George Taylor Richardson Memorial Fund.

In Spirit was the creation that forged an artistic alliance between Tara Beagan and Andy Moro, and is now their company ARTICLE 11's creative property.

NOTES

the reality of this story

This play would not exist if not for the courage of those who remain. With the blessing of a relative who survived great loss, I have undertaken the creation of this play to honour her daughter and the effects that the grievous loss of a life and of lost potential can have on a community. Names and identifying details have been changed.

Every missing and murdered person has her own story. This is one fictionalized account inspired by all too many true stories.

place

The Ntlaka'pamux word for Grannie is *Yuh'*yuh. The accent is on the first syllable and there is a glottal stop between syllables, which is noted with the apostrophe.

design

All non-textual elements appear either as SOUND, LIGHT, or VIDEO. When they appear without a space between the lines, they take place concurrently. Similarly, when they appear before or after a stage direction, they take place as that action takes place. The Super 8 segments are the size of a large 1970s television screen.

language

Molly is an extremely intelligent twelve-year-old, yet she still has her doubts in this adult world. These doubts manifest in "upspeak," or in sentences that sound like questions—they go up in pitch toward the end—even if they are statements. They are noted with a question mark in parentheses following a sentence, like so.(?) Further, Molly struggles to understand her world, so her thoughts often trail off. When she can intuit the end of the thought but cannot bear to speak it, the end of the thought appears in parentheses . . . (like so). Occasionally, the beginning of a thought appears in parentheses because she is searching for the assembly of a thought. (Exactly) like so.

characters

Molly, twelve years old

The side of a road.

Bicycle parts are scattered about.

There is a large weather-worn billboard, long ago stripped of any advertisement.

VIDEO: Flashes on the billboard, full screen.

SOUND: Static.

The slow, eerie "turn the page when you hear the chimes" bell sound.

Subtly, beneath this sound, is the sound of whimpering. So softly we feel it may be us making the sound.

VIDEO: Full screen, the partial sunlight of an eclipse glows as Molly emerges from the spectator area and into the light of the emerging sun. It distorts and vibrates, as from a bad television signal.

Molly does not know where or how she is. A moment while she drops in, adjusts, and takes in the situation.

When she speaks her voice is out of sync, like a corrupt video file or delayed TV broadcast.

MOLLY
Light. But no warmth.

> *The light is still only from the video—cool and white. She turns to see us.*

Are you . . . hello?

Can you see me? Who's . . . ?

> *Beat.*

Where is this?

> *Beat.*

Feels like I'm in trouble. HELLO?

> *MOLLY can hear her voice is off. Somehow.*

If you can hear me, we can talk. Feels like I been lonely.

Do I know youse? I'm Molly. I was just . . .

She glances around . . . what was she just doing?

She notices she is in an unknown place. She surveys the space.

This is not my house. Not the garage. I don't know where (we are) . . . I don't think real things happen here. Am I real? Just kidding.

She wasn't.

I can figure it out. I'm Molly.

She resolves to be heard.

(striding forth) I live with my mom and dad and brothers and sisters in a red house by the road.

SOUND: The mechanical sound of something powering down.

MOLLY covers her eyes/face from the light.

The lights bring MOLLY a realization.

LIGHT: The video fades and a warm glow of light comes up on Molly.

I'm in grade six. I'm twelve—almost thirteen. Wait. So. *(maths)* So I . . .

*She has no ability to figure out what today is. An exasper-
ated sigh.*

Sorry. I don't . . .

She looks up to where the clear blue sky should be.

Where's . . . ?

She closes her eyes and holds her arms out.

Beat.

MOLLY *opens her eyes and smiles an uncertain smile at us.*

Do you see me? Feels like you're looking about me. But not really
at me. I don't really get it, but that's . . .

She sighs.

You're so quiet. Did you need some peace and quiet? Adults are
always saying that. They "just need some peace and quiet." They're
not always the same thing, that "peace" and "quiet." I know that
much. Grade six. Twelve. Pretty grown up. From when I was a
kid. I don't . . . I don't remember growing up. Not really.

Beat.

But do we? Do people remember that? Growing?

Only when it hurts, maybe.

My brother sometimes wakes up at night cuzza the growing pains in his legs. I guess he'll be taller than me.

She stomps like a giant for a few steps.

I remember when I lost my first tooth!

VIDEO: Super 8 video of a small girl's gaping tooth hole.

And the second one there—right beside it. Big space for a while. Could put a straw in it. I guess I lost all the baby teeth eventually, but I don't remember checking for tooth fairy money every time. Only those first two or three. Can't remember stuff I know I musta been there for. Stuff I was there for! When I turned ten I got a dog I didn't want.

VIDEO: Super 8 video of an excitable young dog.

Not that I don't super love dogs, but it's just because we live by the road, and we—anyways. I didn't mean to talk about that. Just saying I remember that birthday present, but not the one from turning eleven, which is funny because eleven was more recent.

SOUND: Bike wheels faintly heard, though at first they sound like a needle running at the end of a record.

For twelve I got my own record player. You gotta treat the needles real gentle or else they stop working, and it's a pain to go buy new ones.

MOLLY kicks a chunk of billboard to reveal the bike frame.

Bike!

I got a bike this year! HA!—Dad. Gave me my birthday present early. Dad, you're too excited to wait. Me, too! Ha, ha! Mom gets after you.

She pulls out the bike frame—only the rear tire is attached— and beholds it.

Whose . . . ? Oh, no. Same colour as my bike. Looks kinda worn out, though. I'm pretty lucky, I got a brand-new bike. This one's nice, too, though, I'm sure, when it's all in one piece, innit?

Got my present seven days early. Easter holidays. But my birthday is at the end of Easter holidays and that would be too crazy, getting a new bike on the last day of holidays!(?) Anyways . . . I'm almost a teenager. Pretty close. I been pretty lucky, though. Mostly people don't treat me like I don't know anything, or say things like, "Oh, you're just a kid," blah blah blah . . . no one at home, anyway. Even the bike I got—it wasn't babyish with streamers or something. I've done lots of stuff. I learned how to sew my own things! I can do it. Could bake all the recipes in your box, almost. Mom.

She searches for her a moment.

In my mom's . . . I mean, if you wanted me to. I could. Yeah. But I . . . I'd like to . . . Do all that stuff again. I don't get why I . . . Hey!

Beat.

Maybe this summer I can help with the nets, hey? Pack up the truck. Unpack the truck. Carry all that stuff down down down to the river. Set up the sleepin' bags and haul out the nets. Stay up late, telling jokes and goin' "shhhhh!" to each other all night long. "You'll scare the fish"—more laughin'. I like that the best. Grown-ups and kids all talking nice. Even Grannie comes. Even though she misses her shows. She's the best at fishing. Right, Yuh'yuh?

She searches the faces a little.

Hm.

Is my family here? Guys?

Beat.

Mom!

She looks around, frantic to see her mom. Then she feels someone else, right behind her—

Yuh'yuh, I thought I . . . hm.

She breathes it out—big girl.

'Kay. It's okay.

Bike. Dad.

*MOLLY sees another piece of buried bike and uncovers it.
Handlebars.*

I left the house to go show Sherry.

Got on my new bike—

*She pretends to get on the bike, though she only holds the
handlebars. She smiles out, proud as anything.*

SOUND: The flashbulb sound from a camera—pop and
high-pitched whine. Not a domestic camera of the era,
but one used perhaps by pathologists to record data.

VIDEO: Full screen: a sun flare that leaves an imprint of
Molly's image on the bike.

The video quickly becomes roadside footage on a sec-
ondary highway.

Molly's shadow lands in the roadside footage.

Was biking back. Just before that hill right before our house, in the curve, there.

SOUND: A truck engine runs and a truck door slams.

MOLLY, startled, drops the handlebars and steps away from them.

Don't usually see many people we don't know on the road. He said he was lost. Couldn't hear him at first; he seemed almost a bit scared. So then I got off my bike and walked closer to hear him.

She mimes stepping off her bike, handlebars still in hand.

I know I'm not supposed to. Know what I thought, though? I thought, "Oh, geez, this guy's gonna try to steal my darn bike, and I only just got it." Thought I was being real smart, leaving it further from that car.(?)

She sets the handlebars down with a jarring clunk that jogs a memory.

Truck. Anyways, he was saying he's lost. Said he was trying to get back to town. Tried to explain to him where it was he was going, but he seemed confused.

Said if I could just help him get back onto the main highway— said he could bring me back to my bike if I showed him myself, in his car—truck.

She sees the front tire, where it rests. She picks it up, which sparks a memory.

VIDEO: Full screen: interior of truck footage.

SOUND: Radio tuning long, landing, tuning, then gone.

I did not want to do that. You don't get into a stranger's truck, and he . . .

She quickly grabs the tire and holds it firmly with two hands.

She holds it up, peering through it. She rotates it in the air, emulating the tuning radio dial and the steering wheel.

VIDEO: Full screen: the truck driving onto a dirt road.

. . . after that, it changed.

Everything. That man . . . something.

VIDEO: Full screen: sun peering through the tops of trees.

She lowers the front tire and begins attaching it to the bike frame.

She's singing as she tightens the tire's nuts, Conway Twitty's "I've Already Loved You In My Mind."

Speaking again, squeezing the tire.

Is kinda flat. Brand new! Needs air, but probly won't hold it. Rubber wears out. Gets useless. Has to, otherwise tire companies would go broke. And that's how come you get tires on a playground sometimes—they're old ones that aren't any good for tractors and eighteen-wheelers anymore. But they're smoother and so better for kids to play on.

She is delighted to find the bicycle bell. As she attaches the bell to the handlebars:

SOUND: Bike wheels run for a few seconds and stop.

(to herself) I was coming home. Coming back from Sherry's house.

She rings the bell, which triggers more sounds/memory.

SOUND: Sound of the bike crashing to the ground.

VIDEO: Full screen: interior of the truck's cab.

Biking back home. For supper. That man . . .

As if in a trance she walks forth toward the truck.

She rings the bell again.

He pulled in there. Fast. Stopped. Fast. Tires spit rocks.

She retreats from the truck.

SOUND: A collection of sounds from her final hour—
truck pulling up on gravelly shoulder, ambient sound of
a man in the cab, radio, etc.

One of her hands releases the handlebars, and they flop down.

SOUND: The bike bell rings again, one time, on its own.

*MOLLY, incredulous, stares at the bell. She tosses the handlebars
aside, far from her.*

VIDEO: Full screen: a man's hand on the truck's steering
wheel.

SOUND: The truck door opens and the man walks toward
Molly, on gravel. We hear Molly's voice say "Hi."

No!

SOUND: A cacophony of brutal noises.

She cowers far from the billboard.

Nononononono.

She jumps up and shouts down the noise.

My name is Molly Arnold and I live in a red house by the road with my mom and dad and brothers and sisters.

SOUND: Has gone.

I go to Central. I'm in the same class as my best friend Sherry. We been best friends since before kindergarten. When we grow up we're gonna live right next door to each other in town. Me 'n' Sherry. She lives just down the road. She has five brothers. Five. Can you imagine how many fights are at that house? But the good thing is that she knows how to fight. She showed me if a guy has you in a headlock like this—you just become dead weight. And he can't hold you up by your head like that 'cause a) too heavy and b) if he ended up breaking your neck your dad would kill him.

She looks to the handlebars and bell.

That's only if someone's worried about getting in trouble, though.

SOUND: Weight being thrown into the back of a covered truck.

If they don't care who does what to them, it's not a good strategy. Some people don't care about trouble. That's when you have to be really, really smart and brave.

MOLLY walks courageously toward the handlebars and bell.

She removes the bell and sets it down firmly, at a bit of a distance.

MOLLY begins to work, attaching the handlebars to the frame.

There's a man who looks at you like he's been your friend for years and years. You think he might say, "I known you since you were only yea high." And you'd have to listen to him tell some story about you when you were little, but there's a chance it wasn't even you. How could he prove it? Could be some other little girl—his niece maybe. Anyways . . . this guy looks like he knows you and then next thing he tells you he doesn't. That he's trying to get to such and such a place and he can't figure out the road signs, and can I help him.

She regards the bike. The handlebars are in place. Hm.
Fair job.

But I don't think you really know how to get somewhere if you don't drive a car yet. Sometimes you only know how to get places by how your mom or dad knows. You can only tell that you kind of know when one of them takes a different turn one time. Then you feel like you just woke up and go, "What? I thought we were going to the arena?" and it turns out you're picking up some neighbour who smells like smokes, but you can't complain 'cause that is so rude, and you want to seem mature. No, you want to be mature.

That's a big thing about being mature. Doing things no matter what your feelings are about doing them. Like always being nice to people. No matter how mean they are to others, usually they are even more mean to themselves. That's what I was told. Yuh'yuh says that people are mean only because they need kindness so bad. So you have to just be brave and be nice even if it seems like it might end up hurting your feelings somehow. Just in case that person really, really needs it soooo bad.

There's something about the bell.

Slowly MOLLY inches toward the bell, picks it up, takes a deep breath, and rings it.

SOUND: A school bell rings for recess and kids play frantically on the playground.

Anthony Voght asked me to be his girlfriend. One day at recess he just walk right up to me and asked. In front of Sherry, Betty, and Maurie. Right out loud. Most people send you a note or their friend asks you for them. But Anthony Voght just walked right up to me and asked. I think maybe he's a little bit nuts. Like there may be problems with his brain. Sherry had this cat that used to try to eat the carpet because of one day when her dad accidentally dropped a pot of stew on its head.

VIDEO: Super 8 video of a cat on carpet, running away.

SOUND: Crossfade into a family dinner cacophony: cutlery on plates, etc.

The stew was dripping a bit from the side, where her dad had made a mess with the spoon, and that cat was licking the drips off the floor. Well, Sherry's family is pretty big and they were all home for supper—their dad's deer stew. He had only given out maybe three or four bowls and so the pot was still real heavy. So that cat is licking the drips and Sherry's dad didn't see him. So he steps on that cat's tail and the cat screams—sounds just like a human baby in great pain—

SOUND: A kettle whistle shrieks.

—and it gave her dad such a scare he dropped that pot BAM onto the cat's head. That cat wriggled out and run away, crying.

SOUND: Dinner sounds are silenced.

Later when they found it, it wasn't dead, but it had some dry blood out its nose. Sherry says ever since then that cat was crazy and tried to eat stuff that wasn't food. Not just carpet, but wood chips and spools of thread and one time a hot water bottle.

Anyways, I told Anthony I couldn't be his girlfriend because I had to be sixteen before I had a boyfriend. My friends teased me 'cause it wasn't true and I was pretty nice about it. So they pretended they thought I loved him, just to tease. I don't care. I don't love him and that's that. He's cute sort of, but I do think he's a bit nuts.

VIDEO: Super 8 video of a boy being bullied on the playground.

And that makes him unpredictable. And so he's not stable, and that's kind of what you want to look for.

A moment.

She walks around the space, seeking something important.

She finds it.

The bike seat. She picks it up.

I gave that man directions, sort of. By saying whose house to turn left at and which farm to go right after, that sort of directions.(?) But the thing is, was he didn't know the families whose names I said and then I tried to tell him the colours of the houses or else describe them good. Um . . . say . . . "When you get to the end of the road, you'll see a big white house, but the main part, which is white, is peeling and looks almost grey 'cause of the old wood underneath. The trim, though, was redone two years ago and it's bright yellow."

Beat.

But no luck, he just looked like he was even more lost. He made jokes, not funny ones, though. Lots of times adults think something's funny, but they can't even explain to you why they're laughing. Seems dumb. Then he asked was I looking for a job this summer.

MOLLY finds wrenches in the tool kit attached to the bike seat. She sets the bike seat down and heads back to the front tire with the wrenches. She tightens the screws.

I babysit my cousins and then my auntie lets me use her sewing machine and gives me a drive into town once a month. We go shopping or sometimes we just look around, if I'm saving up. Don't need a job yet, not yet. I only tell him, "No, thank you." This man says he's got a new company opening up—needs teenagers to work there. He thinks even though I'm young I could learn really well and then stay on every summer until I grow up and move on to a new job.

At first he seems pushy in a nice kind of way. Like those teachers who seem to think you're smarter than you are.(?) But anyways, he doesn't need to know my whole life, so I just said it again, "No, thank you."

> SOUND: Under the following, the radio in the truck plays Conway Twitty with a looping reverb.

I think of Anthony and how he smiled even when I said for the third time that I could not become his girlfriend. This man's eyes did the same thing. His smile kept going, but his eyes sort of went serious for a second. Something about that is scary, when it's in real life. Like they know the reason to smile is over, but what else can he do? He already has the smile on.

> SOUND: The Conway Twitty loop ends abruptly with a truck door slam.

Like news people at the end of the news.

> VIDEO: A TV frames Molly's face.

"Good night."

Demonstrates news people holding a smile.

And how they keep shuffling the papers there . . .

Demonstrates this as well.

Then maybe do this—

She changes her hand positions on the desk before her, then laughs.

And you just wish they'd put the commercial on already, poor guys.

VIDEO: The TV frame snaps away.

I love that part. That's the one part I really like to catch. My dad, he's there, watching the whole news, but I just go over for that last part after the last commercials.

VIDEO: A large 1970s wood-panelled TV set appears, resting on the ground. On it is footage of a hand tuning a radio, interrupted by static and then footage of the RCMP musical ride.

I sit right beside my dad's legs on the carpet there.

One time after supper, me and my mom were doing dishes and I asked her how come you never see Indians on the news unless it's because some white men are mad about something Indians did that hurt "The Economy." Then I mentioned that it seems like "The Economy" is more important than . . . people! And than everything for those white men on the news. Anyways, my mom looked at me kind of like she was going to laugh or ask me something, but instead she just smiled, all proud, and said, "Molly." Then she called my dad in and got me to say it all over again. That time, the way they smiled at me together, I could feel they thought I was growing up. I guess that's one way how we know we're growing without measuring by pains or clothes.

As she feels her shirt, she remembers something about the man.

"You're a cutie," he said. And I didn't say nothing.

SOUND: Static.

VIDEO: The TV goes away and the screen fills with static.

Full screen: It crossfades to blurry, fast motion, chaotic road footage.

I know that you don't get into a car of someone who you never met before—truck. First I gave him directions and then I tell him I don't need any summer job—twice. Then he asked me is my dad on welfare, maybe he might want the job. And this time, when he asked me that, his whole face was smiling but it was all over a really mean smile. It made me just be quiet. Then he said just kidding, but he wasn't.

The full screen road footage fades to black and the 1970s TV returns. *The National* is on.

MOLLY looks for her dad again. She speaks out earnestly, hoping he is there.

I didn't even feel like telling him you work hard. And when you come home sometimes you fall asleep in your chair but still, after supper, you'll take us out to the lake sometimes or to the rink. No point. Some people, there's no point telling them anything real.

MOLLY turns the bike upside down, tires up, balancing on its seat slot and handlebars. She spins the hovering front tire.

(with a sweeping arm gesture) "Diameter." In grade nine you take geometry—my sister Mary Anne was doing some homework and I looked at it. It looked really simple because of the drawings, but there's probably more to it than that. Otherwise we'd be taking it in grade two.

One time in grade four I drew the perfect circle. I still have it, it's on the cover of a scribbler. Butch said I just traced a nickel, but I didn't. Often girls get their periods in grade nine. Anyway, that's what Sherry said. My sister would never say that word at all—"period"? She'd die. I asked her if she wears her bra to bed and she turned so red I thought if we were outside her head might steam. I wouldn't mind a bra. Some of the girls in my class already have bras, but there's only two of them like that. Funny how we get boobs way before we would ever need them.

When I get a bra, I'll probably wear an undershirt still. Or . . . yeah. An undershirt still. Or maybe not. Maybe I'll change a lot from being twelve to being thirteen. Fourteen. Mary Anne used to love her bike like crazy. And now she doesn't even ride it. She walks everywhere probly so people might think she just parked her car pretty far away. Lots can change.

She braves the seat, picking it up gently.

SOUND: The sound of the truck idling, and the Conway Twitty on the radio.

VIDEO: Full screen: sun flashing through trees, the viewer in motion and then stopping suddenly. Sun shining through trees, in motion, faster than is natural.

Told him I had to get home. That man . . . he jumped out of his truck, then, but not closing his door. Just WUSHT! and he was right there, looking at my front tire. He reached out with very dirty hands and squished it—two hard fingers pinching. Said it needed air. Told him I only just got it. And . . .

SOUND: A blunt trauma sound.

MOLLY briefly goes limp and involuntarily drops the seat, her body having responded to a hard blow.

SOUND: Sound of the bike being thrown and landing. Sounds of a mean old dog barking, far off. The truck engine and radio with the Conway Twitty song persists, now distorted.

Right straight up that hill there and up to Old Mae's yard is Rex. Rex the super dog who bites only strangers. He got that man scared. Just for a sec. I saw. Good old Rex.

SOUND: The listener goes into a can.

VIDEO: Full screen: Footage of the tops of trees zipping by—the view from someone lying in the truck bed, facing the sky. The footage skips and scrolls as though the film is off the reel.

You wouldn't know he can barely walk. Sounds like a real killer dog—head made of rusty traps!

VIDEO: Fades as though the viewer blacks out.

Rex knows.

SOUND: Small sounds of pain from Molly, in the back of the truck. The truck radio is off, the truck driving swiftly. The barking gets further and further away.

MOLLY sits with the bike seat and hugs herself. She looks to her wounded bike.

Looks just like mine.

SOUND: Molly's pained whimpers transition into the sounds of a whimpering wounded dog.

We never kept a dog for more than a year, even. Young dogs get so excited about everything, so before they even know better than to stay off the road they've been run over. Dogs, unlike humans, don't always know better. Wull . . . s'posed to know better. Sometimes adults are pretty dumb. Sorry. I don't mean to be mean.

But come on! Even my teachers, some of them. I mean, most of them were nice. Are nice. This one new teacher said something that makes me feel like furniture once, "You're a NAYTIVE, Molly?" 'cause she says it like that 'cause she isn't. "A Nay-tive"— ha! She says, "You're a NAYTIVE, Molly? My goodness, you're so pretty. I thought maybe you were Spanish or Italian." I dunno . . . maybe she didn't mean to be mean, but that's the kind of thing where I almost say out loud, "You should know better." But I don't. But I think it. And sometimes when I think something so mouthy, I laugh right out loud about it. And I know Yuh'yuh would get after me for it, but she might laugh, too!

Possibly people, like dogs, are only mean when the people who raise them are mean.

I tried to train those dogs. All of them. I tried, and I was kind. And we do keep them tied up for a long time until it seems like they know. Somehow it always ends up bad like that. Many dead dogs. Must be doing something wrong.

*There are tiny shards of plywood billboard on the stage,
having broken off of the corners.* MOLLY *slowly tries to fix
the billboard pieces as she tells this.*

How many times does your own dog die before you stop crying
about it? I've had . . . Max. Wilma. Trudeau. Henderson. Snoopy.
Bongo. Mush—oh, poor Mush. Gravel. And then Trudeau again.
'Member, Mom, you said to give him another chance.

Held silence.

Every time.

Beat.

But actually, when I was . . . hm . . . it was when we had Mush,
so . . . when I was nine! I started hiding for that type of cry.
The kind where probably people would say, "Oh, geez, Molly,
you should know better." 'Cause even though you do, you still
feel bad. Or sad. You can't help it. Anyways . . . I didn't want
any more dogs since that last time . . . the second Trudeau. That
same time the second Trudeau got ran over and so quickly we
got Mush, Sherry's dog Buffy ran away. I didn't say to Sherry,
but I kinda thought that was lucky. At least she could imagine
Buffy was somewheres else. You could just be in the yard and
maybe she'd just run right back home: "Buffy! I never seen you
since you were yea high!"

She tries to laugh, but can't.

I guess that's about the time when most kids try not to cry. Nine years old. Grade four or so . . . when you're little you want people to see you cry, to get things. Attention, a Band-Aid, someone else in trouble, a treat maybe. But then we get a bit bigger and we try to not cry.

There's a kid in my class who cried about falling over—a boy. Well, I guess it was a bit more than just falling over. Sharon Collins pulled his chair out—

She quickly scans the crowd to make sure the boy isn't present. He isn't.

. . . it was C.J. Swakum! And he plopped right hard onto the hard, hard floor with his butt bones and clipped his chin off the desktop. He screamed with his lips closed, sounded like a kettle whistle.

She does the sound.

SOUND: A quick shrill of a school's fire alarm.

And blood leaked out the front of his mouth. But then he wouldn't open his mouth to show the teacher if his tongue was bit off or what. It wasn't, though. Just bit partway on the bottom— right across there. That would kill, though. Teeth mark cuts on the bottom of your tongue? Geez. But he didn't need stitches or anything and he cried and cried. He could only eat soup for a while, to be careful of his injury.

The teacher didn't see who done it and neither did C.J., but us kids all did. So she takes C.J. to the nurse and tells us all, "Do not move a hair." Then she comes back and goes:

VIDEO: Super 8 quality. Teacher's hands in judgment.

"Who did this? WHO DID THIS?" and we could tell Sharon was gonna be dead meat. But, see, Sharon was only doing it for a joke and because C.J. does stuff like that all the time—runs in the halls, talks without raising his hand, and really bullies kids in smaller grades. None of us probably even thought Sharon should get in trouble for it, so nobody said. And Sharon just sat there, looking a bit like she was frozen. Finally the bell rings and the teacher goes, "Nobody is leaving this room until I find out who did this." And some kids looked right at Sharon, and some just looked down. Felt like a hundred years. Nobody says nothing! Then, slowly, slowly, Sharon just stands up. Didn't make a peep, only stands. And teacher goes, "Thank you, Sharon." She got in so much trouble in front of everyone but she didn't cry one bit. And we all felt a bit guilty because we laughed so hard at C.J.—until we saw the blood. All down his shirt here. And it was picture day! But thank goodness our grade already had our pictures done in the morning. I think if I was C.J. I wouldn't have cried, but if I was Sharon I would have secretly cried later, in my room after my mom and dad had to get me in trouble all over again.

She glances at the bike. She walks over to it and kneels down beside it.

Actually . . . I'm not Sharon or C.J., but for some reason I still did cry about that. Not a big deal, but just a little. In private. It just seemed upsetting to me for some reason.

Ugh, that picture—

(to audience again) Didn't even know it was picture day.

> VIDEO: Molly's school picture flashes up, patchy and incomplete.

Mary Anne found out I took her shirt 'cause of that—picture day. Geez. Got caught red-handed! Anyway, she woulda let me if I just asked.

> *She looks for Mary Anne in the audience, to no avail.*

Sorry, Mary Anne.

> *Beat.*

School picture. Feels lonely.

(panicked) Mom?

> VIDEO: Full screen: gently, wind in trees.

> SOUND: Wind in trees.

She feels Yuh'yuh's soft, warm hand on her shoulder, turns to see her.

Hey, Yuh'yuh. You here? Grannie? I feel like you really are. (Beside me.) Right here.

She goes to the bike seat.

Henderson lived three weeks less than a year—I really thought he was gonna make it. So close, so close. Still . . . he held the record for ages. We got him right after Canada won a big hockey game against commies—my brother Butch named him, but he loved me the most. He was pretty much my dog. I was . . . eight. By the time he died, though, I was nine. Summer holidays.

Everyone was playing outside before we had our barbecue, but I wanted to see the whole news that day, to see the solar eclipse on TV that a cameraman got. I was sitting in my dad's chair, which almost never happens, but he was outside watching my mom run the barbecue and passing her things like tongs and a flipper. My brother ran in for a sec to grab his mitt and find a baseball. He said it seems dumb to watch the sun on TV when it's right here outside anyway. I said it wasn't the same but I didn't bother explaining because he should know better anyway. Henderson was sitting on my feet, all sleepy and good. My brother asked could Henderson come outside with him. He was good at grabbing baseballs that went haywire. The eclipse was about to come on, so I said go ahead and take him just so he'd get. Of course Henderson would go only if I asked him to, so I did, for the sake of my brother. "Go on, Henderson! Go play outside," and they went.

The commercials are just ending and I hear my mom shout, "BUTCH THE DOG!" which makes me laugh because it sounds like she's calling Butch a dog, and Butch does sound like a dog name.

Then it's very quiet outside . . . and then I realize.

SOUND: A high-pitched ringing—the bike bell slowed down and driven up in pitch.

And they finally show the eclipse—they're gonna show all six minutes. I stare at the eclipse and I don't look outside where everyone must be looking in to see if I saw what happened.

SOUND: Shovel-digging sound.

I hear Mom say, "My God, Butch. Get him into a flour sack before Molly sees him." And someone goes running in the back door and down to the basement to find a bag big enough for a dog. And I hear someone else go into the shed. For the shovel.

Beat.

MOLLY finds the bell and the seat. She runs up to the billboard and does a demonstration, with the bell as the moon and the seat as the sun. She enjoys her shadow show on the billboard.

VIDEO: Full-screen whiteout.

An eclipse happens when the moon is sitting between the sun and us. Normally the sun is on one side of us and the moon on the other, and at night the sun shines on the moon from way over there, making it seem bright. Moonlight is actually made of sunlight. During a solar eclipse everything is where it's not supposed to be all at once and what you see is only the brightest light from the sun that couldn't get blocked out. The sun is so much bigger than the moon it's not even funny. And so . . . you know it's still there—the sun—even though it seems like the world has gone dark. I saw the brightest outline of sun shine out onto Earth. And I remember I felt like that chair I was sitting in felt big.

MOLLY steps away from the billboard where she was doing the eclipse demonstration.

VIDEO: A black and white image of her—ghostly faint and life-size—remains on the screen, watching her in-person self walk away. The image of her fades slowly.

Six minutes ended and the news people came back on. But before they started doing their smiles I closed my eyes and held the picture of the eclipse in my eyelids—glowing green—different colour, same shape. I could feel my feet were still warm from where Henderson was layeen there. I could hear someone walking quietly into the house—shutting the screen door really gentle, each click slow slow slow. I figured it was my mom coming to tell me that my dog is dead again. But I stayed with my eyes closed anyways. She came close to me and I realized by how quiet she stayed that she thought I was sleeping.

MOLLY treats the bike the way her mom treats her in the story, lifting it gently and laying down with it to rest.

Even though I was already nine she scooped me up and carried me to my bed, like a little kid. And it was kind of babyish but also nice. When she was gone I cried onto my pillow. Light blue went dark blue in one wet blob. I fell asleep a little.

She sits up.

I came outside on time for the coals to be good for marshmallows. No hot dog for me, just marshmallows.

VIDEO: Full screen: close-up on fire coals, embers.

At bedtime, when my mom tucked me in for the second time in one day, I cried again. But I said it was 'cause of my sore stomach. Moms can take care of a sore stomach.

She speaks out to her mom, somewhere, in the house.

We both knew I was only just upset. Then you brang me crackers and ginger ale and talked to me until my crying and crackers was done. And I fell asleep.

She soothes the bike seat.

Sherry's grannie says dogs don't have a spirit. But, no. She's wrong. Everything does. Yuh'yuh said I should have a funeral for Henderson still even though I was sick of them. Said it would let him go. Let me let him go. 'Member?

She knows her grandmother is there now. Somehow, somewhere.

She helped me do a funeral, too. Yuh'yuh. Even though it was during her shows. We did the funeral, and I was sad; I couldn't help it. Grannie says that's part of it. But . . . the thing was I felt mad too, and then I felt bad about being mad, and so I was just crying real hard. Harder than ever. Of course Grannie asked me what was going on. Because . . . what happened was I realized— all those times our dogs run out on the road? All those times they done that and got ran over? Well, the car that hit them—someone was driving that car. Truck. But do you think one of them even stopped to see what it was they ran over? Pull over? Take a good look at what they done and come tell us? Say sorry at least? Not even. Not even once! And sometimes for sure other people saw what happened, and they didn't say nothing either.

Beat.

So that's why I was mad.

Silence.

Grannie says we have to forgive those people. But I haven't figured that one out yet. Dumb. But, so—we had Henderson's funeral. And there was lots of crying. Out of me. Grannie said prayers in Indian, really soft. And she got us kids to tell stories about Henderson. It was hard but important. When we was done, the wind came and swirled around all of us and went shuwush-hhh up the trees.

VIDEO: Full screen: fire sparks whooshing upward.

Yuh'yuh said it's Henderson's spirit going. Freefree.

And things kept going, just how they always were. Have supper. Homework. Go to bed. Wake up—have breakfast, but don't feed Henderson, like I always used to.

MOLLY holds the seat again, as though it is Henderson's head.

Go to school, come home, don't feed Henderson again. Go to Sherry's, come home, have supper, on and on how we do. And eventually you think of not feeding Henderson, not playing with him, not feeling his softie ears less and less.

After feeling its softie ears, MOLLY attaches the seat.

Mournfully she sings the Conway Twitty song again.

The bike is complete but for the bell. She stands the bike up, showing it to the audience.

My bike had a kickstand.

MOLLY sees the kickstand is there.

She lowers the kickstand and lets the bike stand on its own.

SOUND: Slow bell chime in reverse.

My bike had a kickstand. Is this my bike?

Hey. Is this my bike?

> *MOLLY finds the bell and picks it up. She rings it, commanding the audience to tell her.*

> VIDEO: TV newscast montage, ending with her missing poster.

Missing.

. . . the whole world. Everything.

> VIDEO: One by one the images we've seen glow up like photos.

Missing. That one day. Everything changed.

Someone knows.

I remember only pieces of things.

> *She attaches the bell to the handlebars.*

He threw that bike like it was nothing.

> *The bike tips over with a crash.*

Felt my throat get thick. Him smiling with serious eyes.

I can't go freefree.

She calms. She knows now.

There is a man who knows what happened.

I only remember small pieces—the brightest ones peeking through—hurts my head.

> MOLLY *moves to the fallen bike to stand over it. She looks at the bike as though she is looking down at herself. She then enacts the man looking over her.*
>
> LIGHT: Becomes harsh and focused behind Molly on the billboard.

There is a man who smiled at me when I cried. I don't know where . . . I could see part of his face; he was bent down low to look at me. Something in his hand. Darker out, but still daytime. The sun's behind him, peeking through the trees and under his ears and over his head.

> SOUND: Molly's voice floats around us.

I can remember it like that—only small peeks of remembering— only the brightest light shining through. I remember . . .

Standing against the billboard now, MOLLY takes the position she describes to us, only standing up.

I felt between my fingers that I was on the dirt. A branch or a rock was poking my head but I couldn't move away from it. I tried to ask him to move that branch please, but only small sounds came out. My mouth felt big and hot, but one side of my face was on the ground—cold and soft. I could see where someone had left their shirt behind, on a stump.

Beat.

I saw where it looked like there was a long piece of long black hair snagged on a bush.

My hair. It's my hair. (My) Shirt. How . . . ?

SOUND: The truck radio plays again. A dog barks, far away.

Grinding on gravel.

MOLLY walks away from the billboard and out of the light.

VIDEO: Her image, lifeless on the ground, remains as live Molly walks away. We see Molly's soul departing her body.

SOUND: A simultaneous roar of an engine, a dog barking, a truck radio, a truck door slamming, horrible cracking sounds.

LIGHT: Darkness engulfs Molly.

SOUND: The truck squeals away.

The truck driving away fades off into the distance.

The end.

ACKNOWLEDGEMENTS

Andy Moro. Seeing your work made me understand how this work could be possible in this life.

Thanks, as ever, to my mom, Pauline Beagan, for keeping every newspaper clipping and photograph relevant to our wee family.

In Spirit, now an ARTICLE 11 project, has partnered with Indigenous companies Saskatchewan Native Theatre Company of Saskatoon (now Gordon Tootoosis Nīkānīwin Theatre) and Urban Indigenous Theatre Company of Winnipeg, creating viable touring productions with artists of each locale. A11 is working toward giving productions to trusted Indigenous companies to get the story of one missing girl up and running far and wide.

Kind thanks to premiere actor Michaela Washburn, whose artistry and heart helped to define my practice. Your spiritual guidance during our debut kept me going, and your talent kept me in awe.

Thanks to Sera-Lys McArthur, who has played Molly in a fly-in reserve gymnasium to twelve people, done staged readings at conferences, and shone as Molly in the full production. Your talent and skill amaze me.

Thanks also to Columpa Bobb, who bore witness to the play three times in Vancouver, and then spoke the wisdom shared by your mother Lee Maracle: "The hardest truths must be spoken gently, and that is what you have done." Thank you for knowing our intentions and inviting us to Urban Indigenous Theatre Company. You are a magnificent leader and artist.

Our community helps us see ourselves, and for that I am eternally grateful.

Support was given by Native Earth Performing Arts as recommenders of the Ontario Arts Council's Theatre Creators Reserve Program. Further development of the play is thanks to Jovanni Sy, then artistic director of Cahoots Theatre Projects, and the Ontario Arts Council's Playwright-in-Residence funding. The play was hosted, in workshop, at the Cahoots Theatre Projects Writer's Retreat at the Shaw Festival in November/December 2007 and January 2009.

Tara Beagan is a proud Ntlaka'pamux and Irish "Canadian" halfbreed based in Calgary, Alberta. She is co-founder/ director of ARTICLE 11 with her most cherished collaborator, Andy Moro. She served as the artistic director of Native Earth Performing Arts from February 2011 to December 2013. A Dora Mavor Moore Award–winning playwright, she has been in residence at Cahoots Theatre, NEPA, the National Arts Centre, and Berton House. Five of her twenty plus plays have been published, and her first film script, *133 Skyway*, co-written with Randy Redroad, won the imagineNATIVE award for best Canadian drama. Beagan is also a Dora and Betty Mitchell Award– nominated actor.

First edition: November 2017
Printed and bound in Canada by Imprimerie Gauvin, Gatineau

Cover photo of Sera-Lys McArthur © Juan Camilo Palacio, and
provided courtesy of Native Earth Performing Arts
Cover design by Andy Moro
Author photo © Andy Moro

**PLAYWRIGHTS
CANADA PRESS**

202-269 Richmond St. W.
Toronto, ON
M5V 1X1

416.703.0013
info@playwrightscanada.com
www.playwrightscanada.com
@playcanpress